EVERYTHING SPORTS ALMANACS

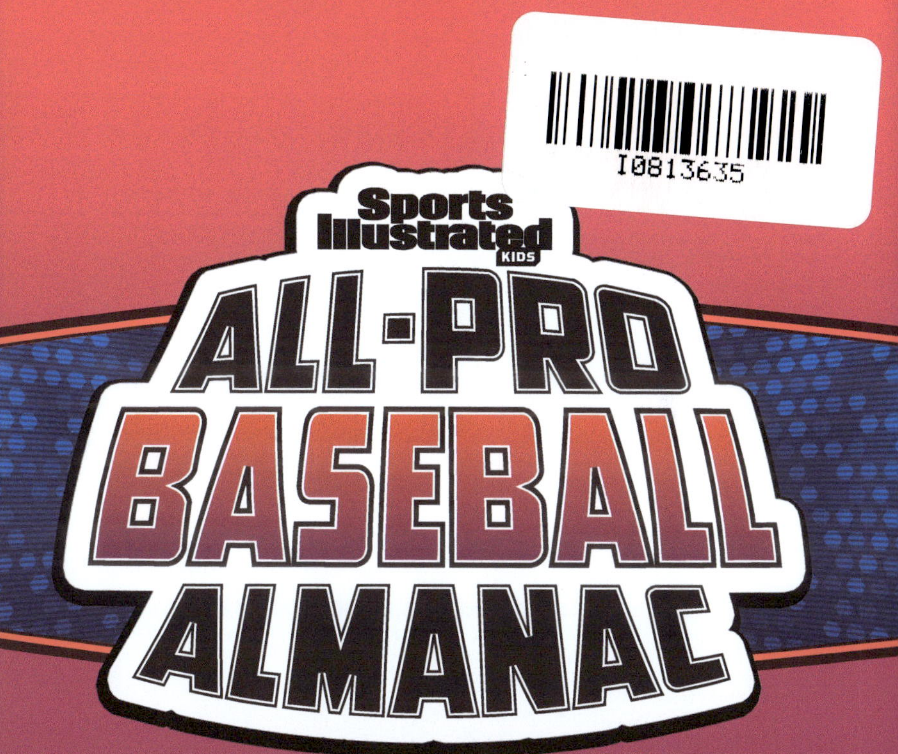

BY PATRICK DONNELLY

CAPSTONE PRESS
a capstone imprint

Published by Capstone Press, an imprint of Capstone
1710 Roe Crest Drive, North Mankato, Minnesota 56003
capstonepub.com

Library of Congress Cataloging-in-Publication Data is available on the Library of Congress website.

ISBN: 9798875232589 (hardcover)
ISBN: 9798875232534 (paperback)
ISBN: 9798875232541 (ebook PDF)

Summary: Exciting pro baseball facts in a variety of formats keep excited sports fans turning the page.

Editorial Credits
Editor: Mandy Robbins; Designer: Sarah Bennett; Media Researcher: Rebekah Hubstenberger; Production Specialist: Tori Abraham

Image Credits
Associated Press: Jim Mone, 17; Getty Images: Chris Arjoon, 33 (top), Chris Coduto, 42, Cole Burston, cover (left), Dustin Satloff, 46 (bottom), Ed Zurga, 41 (bottom), Elsa, 12, Ezra Shaw, 13, 14 (bottom), iStock/envastudio (dots), throughout, Jed Jacobsohn, 35 (middle), Jesse D. Garrabrant, 45, Jim McIsaac, cover (right), Kevork Djansezian, 32, Keystone, 9 (middle), 44, Keystone View Company/Archive Photos, 8 (bottom), Luke Hales, 43 (bottom), Mark Rucker/Transcendental Graphics, 28 (top right), Matt Thomas/San Diego Padres, 22 (middle), Michael Reaves, 11, New York Daily News Archive, 18, Nick Cammett, 47 (bottom), Sean M. Haffey, 26, Steph Chambers, cover (top), 4-5; Library of Congress: Prints and Photographs Division, 28 (middle left), 34 (top); Shutterstock: Arrobani Studio, 28 (gold background), Barks, 39, Bonny Munandar (blue background), 41, 44, Dean zangirolami, 43 (top right), Debby Wong, 20, Fallen Knight (holographic background), cover and throughout, ghenadie (gold sparkle background), 19, 29, 31, LIORIKI, 37, Marcio Jose Bastos Silva, 10, Maria Bell (baseball), 7, 11, 33, mentalmind (stars), 29, 30, moondes, 29 (baseball diamond), My Portfolio (baseball stitching), 25, 38, okili77, 47 (top), Oleksii Sidorov, 27 (background), Olga Moonlight, 3, 6-7, rvika, 14-15 (background), Sensvector (baseball), back cover,16, 27, Somchai Som, 34-35 (background), Stacy Nazelrod, 10-11 (background), StarLine, back cover (background), Steinar, 31 (rings), theerakit, 19 (baseball diamond), Tony Oshlick, 6 (hot dog character), Tood House, 23, (baseball player silhouettes), Winner Creative, 8-9 (background); Sports Illustrated: David E. Klutho, 21, John G. Zimmerman, 36, John Iacono, 40, Manny Millan, 24, Neil Leifer, 38, Mark Kauffman, 30 (bottom)

*** All stats are current through March 2025. ***

Printed in the United States 6596

Table of Contents

About the League

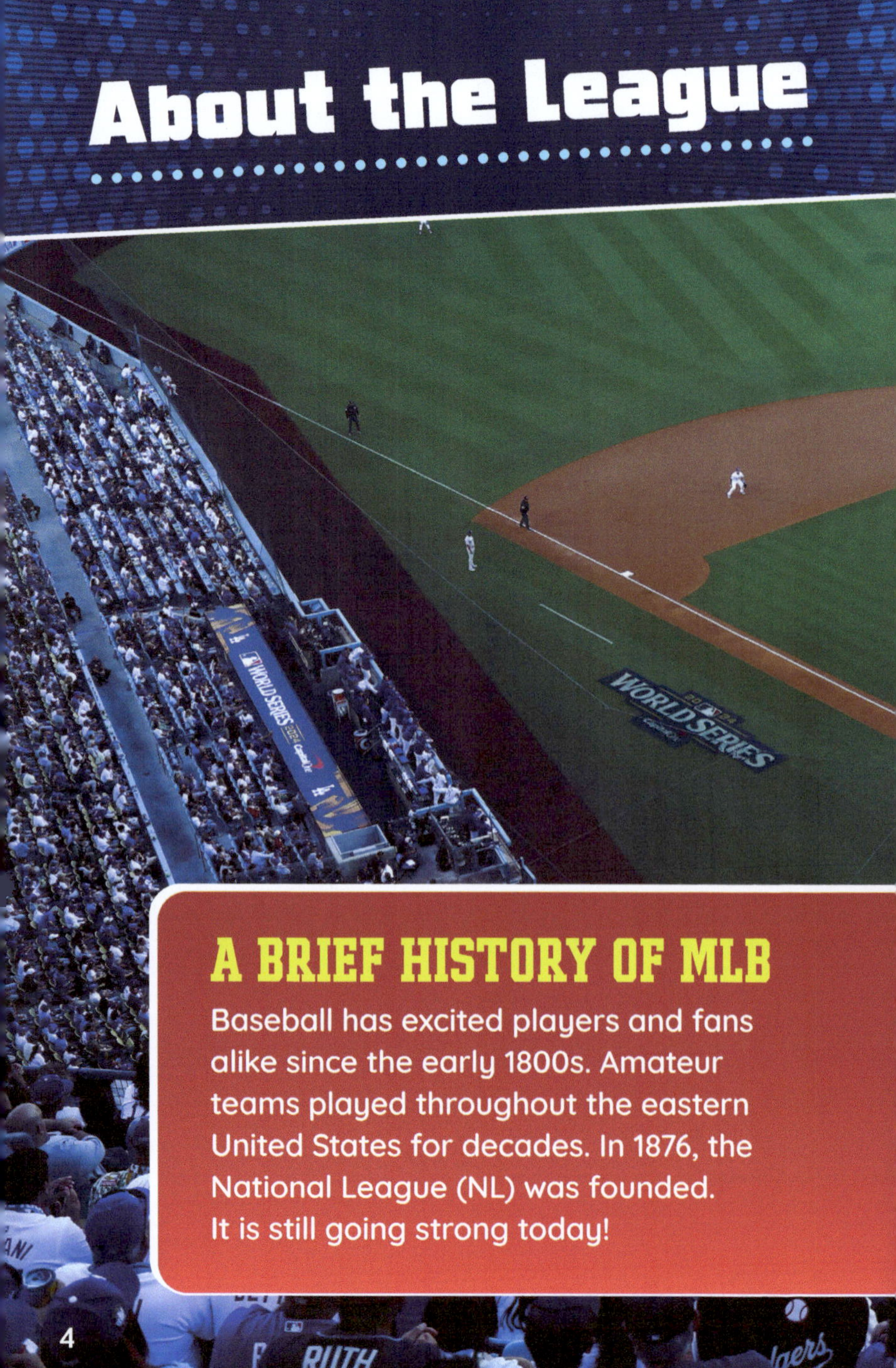

A BRIEF HISTORY OF MLB

Baseball has excited players and fans alike since the early 1800s. Amateur teams played throughout the eastern United States for decades. In 1876, the National League (NL) was founded. It is still going strong today!

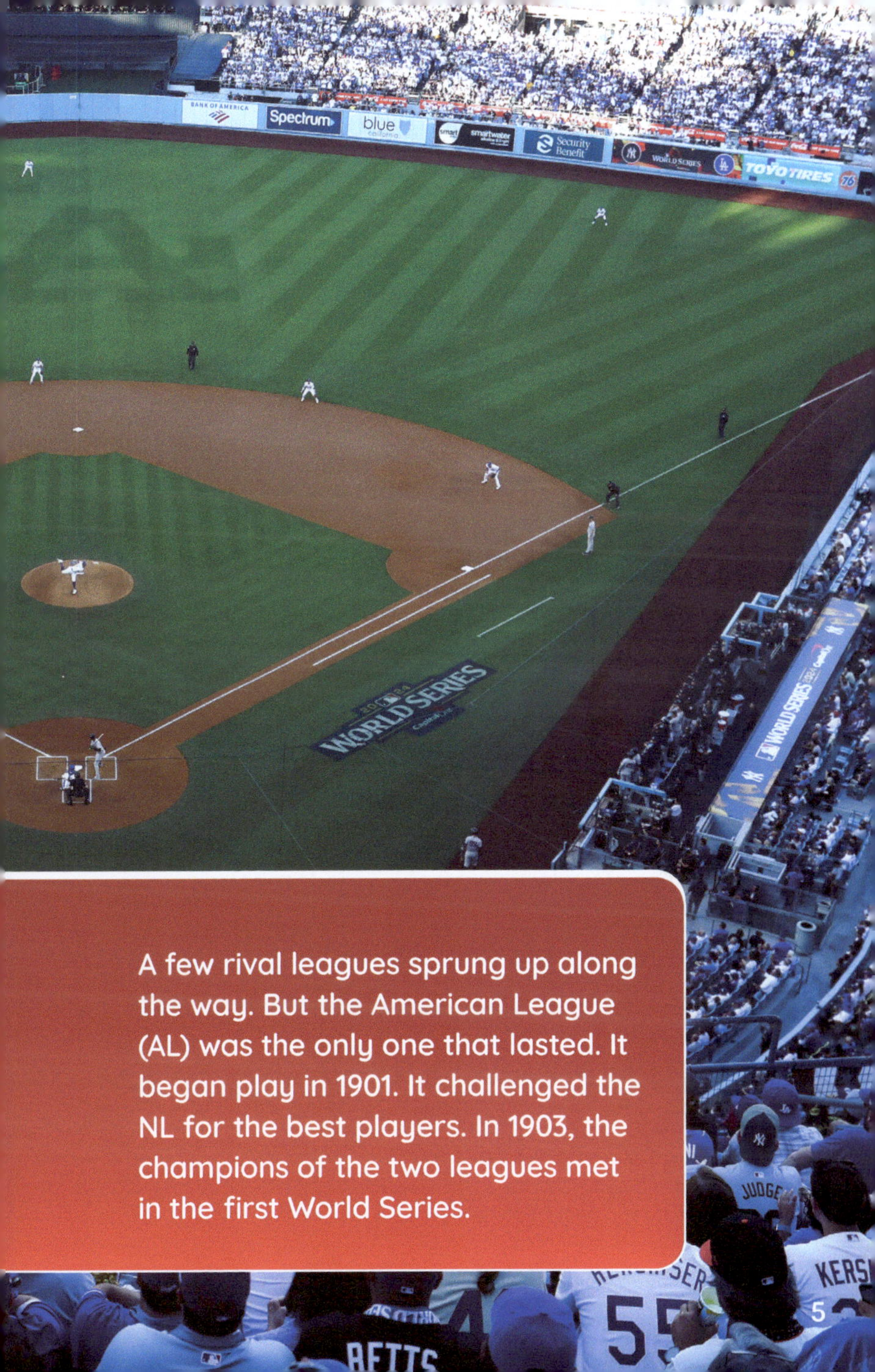

A few rival leagues sprung up along the way. But the American League (AL) was the only one that lasted. It began play in 1901. It challenged the NL for the best players. In 1903, the champions of the two leagues met in the first World Series.

Meet the Teams

NATIONAL LEAGUE

Arizona Diamondbacks
Chase Field
Phoenix, Arizona

Atlanta Braves
Truist Park
Atlanta, Georgia

Chicago Cubs
Wrigley Field
Chicago, Illinois

Cincinnati Reds
Great American Ball Park
Cincinnati, Ohio

Colorado Rockies
Coors Field
Denver, Colorado

Los Angeles Dodgers
Dodger Stadium
Los Angeles, California

Miami Marlins
loanDepot park
Miami, Florida

Milwaukee Brewers
American Family Field
Milwaukee, Wisconsin

New York Mets
Citi Field
Flushing, New York

Philadelphia Phillies
Citizens Bank Park
Philadelphia, Pennsylvania

Pittsburgh Pirates
PNC Park
Pittsburgh, Pennsylvania

San Diego Padres
Petco Park
San Diego, California

San Francisco Giants
Oracle Park
San Francisco, California

St. Louis Cardinals
Busch Stadium
St. Louis, Missouri

Washington Nationals
Nationals Park
Washington, D.C.

AMERICAN LEAGUE

Athletics*
Sutter Health Park
Sacramento, California

Baltimore Orioles
Oriole Park at Camden Yards
Baltimore, Maryland

Boston Red Sox
Fenway Park
Boston, Massachusetts

Chicago White Sox
Rate Field
Chicago, Illinois

Cleveland Guardians
Progressive Field
Cleveland, Ohio

Detroit Tigers
Comerica Park
Detroit, Michigan

Houston Astros
Minute Maid Park
Houston, Texas

Kansas City Royals
Kauffman Stadium
Kansas City, Missouri

Los Angeles Angels
Angel Stadium
Anaheim, California

Minnesota Twins
Target Field
Minneapolis, Minnesota

New York Yankees
Yankee Stadium
Bronx, New York

Seattle Mariners
T-Mobile Park
Seattle, Washington

Tampa Bay Rays
Tropicana Field
St. Petersburg, Florida

Texas Rangers
Globe Life Field
Arlington, Texas

Toronto Blue Jays
Rogers Centre
Toronto, Ontario, Canada

The Las Vegas Athletics?

* The Oakland Athletics announced in 2023 that they would be moving again. They agreed to relocate to Las Vegas, Nevada, starting with the 2027 season.

Story of the Negro Leagues

In its earliest days, organized baseball welcomed Black players. But in the 1880s, race-based segregation became the norm. Black players formed their own teams. They traveled around the country playing games. But they didn't have a league to call their own.

In 1920, the Negro National League was founded. Other leagues came and went. The Negro American League began play in 1937.

»Pedro Ballester scores for the New York Cubans against the Homestead Grays during a 1948 Negro National League game.

The Negro leagues thrived. Then Jackie Robinson debuted with the Brooklyn Dodgers in 1947. MLB was no longer segregated. The best Black players joined MLB teams. The Negro leagues faded out in the late 1950s.

»Jackie Robinson, 1951

OLDEST BALLPARKS STILL IN USE

Park	Team	First Year
Fenway Park	Red Sox	1912
Wrigley Field	Cubs	1914
Dodger Stadium	Dodgers	1962
Angel Stadium	Angels	1966
Kauffman Stadium	Royals	1973

Interleague Play

The NL and AL were completely separate leagues. They only came together for the World Series. In the 1990s, baseball was losing fans. Interleague play was added in 1997. It gives fans a chance to see all the best players every year.

GAME 7
2016 WORLD SERIES

In 2016, the Chicago Cubs went to the World Series for the first time since 1945. They faced Cleveland. The Cubs hadn't won the World Series since 1908. The teams split the first six games. Game 7 in Cleveland would decide the championship. Here's how it went down:

- The **Cubs** led 6–3 in the eighth inning.
- **Cleveland** rallied to tie it.
- **Chicago's Ben Zobrist** hit a two-run double in the 10th inning.

- **Cleveland** brought the tying run to the plate in the bottom of the inning.
- But the **Cubs** got the last out to win 8–7.
- The long wait for a title was over for Cubs fans!

»Cubs players celebrate their 2016 World Series win!

The Longest Game

On May 1, 1920, the Brooklyn Robins played the Boston Braves in the longest game in MLB history. The Robins (soon to be renamed the Dodgers) scored in the fifth inning. The Braves tied it in the sixth. Then nobody scored for the next 20 innings! The game was called after 26 innings due to darkness. Stadium lights had not been invented yet, so the game ended in a 1–1 tie.

»Thanks to modern stadium lighting, games can last well after sunset.

LONGEST MLB GAMES

INNINGS	DATE	TEAMS AND RUNS
26	May 1, 1920	Brooklyn Robins 1 Boston Braves 1
25	May 8, 1984	Chicago White Sox 7 Milwaukee Brewers 6
25	September 11, 1974	St. Louis Cardinals 4 New York Mets 3
24	April 15, 1968	Houston Astros 1 New York Mets 0
24	July 21, 1945	Detroit Tigers 1 Philadelphia Athletics 1
24	September 1, 1906	Philadelphia Athletics 4 Boston Americans 1

THE COVID BUBBLE

The Los Angeles Dodgers once won the World Series without winning a game at home or on the road. How was that possible? During the COVID-19 pandemic of 2020, MLB played most of its postseason games at neutral sites. The Dodgers played every playoff and World Series game at Globe Life Park, home of the Texas Rangers.

GAME 7
1991 WORLD SERIES

The 1991 World Series was known as the "worst to first" series. Both the Minnesota Twins and Atlanta Braves had finished in last place in 1990. But they bounced back to win their leagues' pennants the next year.

Minnesota won the first two games at home.

The Braves won the next three in Atlanta.

The Twins took Game 6 back in Minneapolis.

In Game 7, Twins pitcher Jack Morris pitched 10 innings. He didn't give up a run. The Braves' pitchers were tough too. The game's only run came on Gene Larkin's single in the bottom of the 10th.

The Twins won 1–0!

»Jack Morris pitches for the Minnesota Twins during the first inning of Game 7 of the 1991 World Series.

Standout Plays

Willie Mays Makes the Catch

Many people think Willie Mays is the greatest player in MLB history. His catch in the 1954 World Series is one of the most famous plays of all time. Cleveland slugger Vic Wertz crushed a pitch to deep center field. Mays raced back on a dead sprint. He looked over his shoulder to track the ball. Then he reached up and caught it with his back still facing home plate.

The Gold Gloves of 2024

The Gold Glove is awarded each year to the best fielder at his position in the American League and National League. Check out the winners for the 2024 season.

Center Field
Brenton Doyle
Daulton Varsho

Right Field
Sal Frelick
Wilyer Abreu

Shortstop
Ezequiel Tovar
Bobby Witt Jr.

Second Base
Brice Turang
Andrés Giménez

Third Base
Matt Chapman
Alex Bregman

First Base
Christian Walker
Carlos Santana

Pitcher
Chris Sale
Seth Lugo

Utility Player
Jared Triolo
Dylan Moore

Catcher
Patrick Bailey
Cal Raleigh

Derek Jeter's FLIP

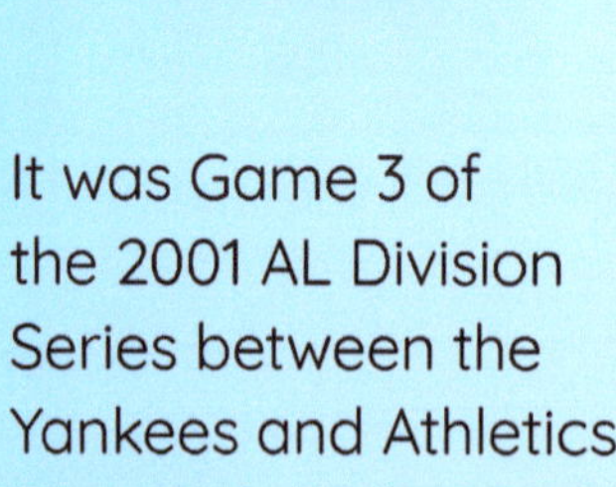

It was Game 3 of the 2001 AL Division Series between the Yankees and Athletics. New York had a 1–0 lead in the seventh inning. Oakland's Jeremy Giambi was on first base with two out. Terrence Long ripped a line drive into the right field corner. Right fielder Shane Spencer grabbed the ball in the corner and fired home.

His throw sailed over the head of the cutoff man. Giambi should have scored easily. But Jeter had raced over from shortstop to back up the play. He caught the ball and back-handed it toward home. Catcher Jorge Posada caught it and tagged Giambi just in time.

DAVID FREESE

Cardinals' third baseman David Freese was the hero of the 2011 World Series. In Game 6, the Rangers were one strike away from winning the title. Then Freese hit a two-run triple to tie the game. He followed that with a game-winning home run in the 11th inning.

» David Freese hits a two-run triple in the ninth inning of Game 6 of the 2011 World Series.

Machado's Triple Play

In 2024, the San Diego Padres needed a win to clinch a playoff spot. They led the Dodgers 4–2 in the ninth inning. But Los Angeles was threatening, with runners on first and second with no outs. Dodgers shortstop Miguel Rojas hit a ground ball. Manny Machado fielded it and stepped on third base. He threw to second for the second out. The relay to first beat Rojas for a triple play!

»Manny Machado of the San Diego Padres tags third base to start a triple play as Miguel Rojas runs to first base.

Unassisted Triple Play

The unassisted triple play is one of the rarest plays in baseball. There have been only 15 of them in MLB history. Most of them happen like this:

Base runners take off as soon as the pitch is thrown.

The batter hits a line drive.

An infielder catches the line drive for the first out.

Then the infielder steps on a base vacated by a runner for the second out.

Then he tags another runner for the third out.

One pitch—three outs!

Five Most Recent MLB *Unassisted* Triple Plays

PLAYER	TEAM AND POSITION	YEAR
Eric Bruntlett	Phillies second baseman	2009
Asdrúbal Cabrera	Cleveland second baseman	2008
Troy Tulowitzki	Rockies shortstop	2007
Rafael Furcal	Braves shortstop	2003
Randy Velarde	Athletics second baseman	2000

Team Dynasties

» The Yankees celebrate winning the 1996 American League Championship.

BRONX BOMBERS

The New York Yankees are the most successful MLB team by far. They've won 27 World Series and have had many legendary players.

Derek Jeter, Bernie Williams, and Andy Pettitte won four World Series rings in the late 1990s.

Reggie Jackson and Ron Guidry led New York to back-to-back titles in 1977 and 1978.

Yogi Berra was part of 10 championship teams from 1947 to 1962.

Joe DiMaggio led the team to nine World Series titles from 1936 to 1951.

Babe Ruth and Lou Gehrig starred in the 1920s and 1930s.

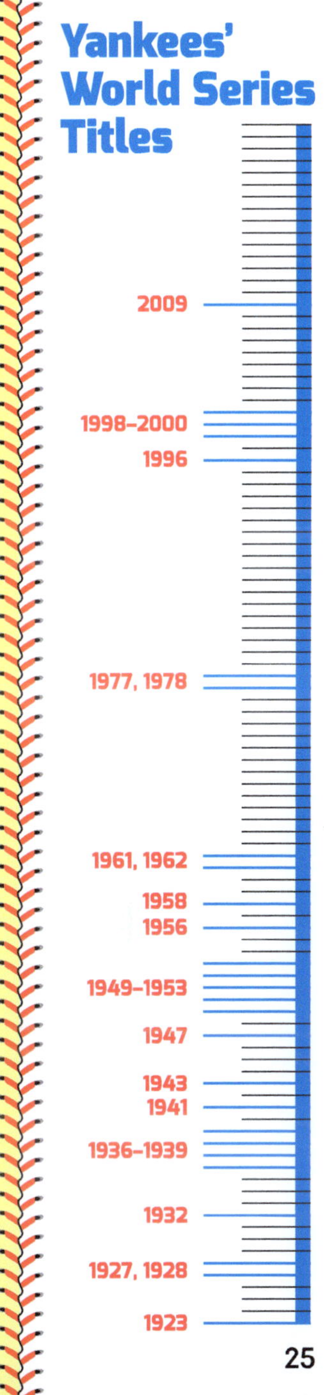

RED SOX RALLY

Since the Yankees' last dynasty ended in 2000, the Boston Red Sox have won four World Series. The championships were spread out—2004, 2007, 2013, and 2018—making it hard to call them a dynasty. In 2004, the Red Sox became the first team to come back from a 3-0 game deficit to win four straight games in a playoff series.

»The Red Sox celebrate their 2018 World Series win over the Los Angeles Dodgers.

Teams with the Most WORLD SERIES TITLES

Negro League Leaders

The "golden era" of the Negro leagues lasted from 1936 to 1948.

The **Homestead Grays** won nine Negro National League titles in that span.

Josh Gibson

Satchel Paige

The **Kansas City Monarchs** won six Negro American League championships.

The Negro World Series was held every year from 1942 to 1948. The Monarchs won the first Negro World Series. But the Grays emerged as the best team from that era. They won three Negro World Series titles.

Former Negro Leaguers in the Hall of Fame

In the 1970s, MLB opened the Hall of Fame to players who spent most or all of their careers in the Negro leagues. Here are the first five Negro leaguers to be inducted.

Monte Irvin
1973 - outfielder

Buck Leonard
1972 - first baseman

James "Cool Papa" Bell
1974 - outfielder

Josh Gibson
1972 - catcher

Satchel Paige
1971 - pitcher

Jackie Robinson's Dodgers

Jackie Robinson integrated MLB when he joined the Brooklyn Dodgers in 1947. During his 10 years with them, they won six NL pennants. In each of those years, the Yankees won the AL title. They met in the World Series six times. The Yankees won five. Brooklyn won its lone title in 1955.

Jackie Robinson

Players with the Most World Series Rings

Not surprisingly, all of the players with the most World Series titles are Yankees.

Yogi Berra tops them all with a whopping 10 World Series rings.

Joe DiMaggio is a close second with nine.

Today, Mookie Betts has the most World Series rings of any active player with three. He won once with the Red Sox and twice with the Dodgers.

Behind him, 21 players are tied for second place with two championship rings.

Iconic Players

All-Star Ohtani

Baseball has had few players like Shohei Ohtani. He left his native Japan to play for the Los Angeles Angels in 2018. Ohtani is known for hitting long home runs. He's also a dominant pitcher. He was named the AL Most Valuable Player (MVP) in 2021 and 2023. At the 2021 All-Star Home Run Derby, he set a record with six 500-foot homers. The next day, he became the first starting pitcher to bat leadoff and earn the victory in the All-Star Game.

Ohtani joined the Dodgers in 2024. He became the first player in MLB history with 50 home runs and 50 stolen bases in a season. And he won his first NL MVP Award.

Six for Six

Ohtani had a game for the ages on September 19, 2024. He went six for six as the Dodgers beat the Marlins 20–4. His six hits included two doubles and three home runs. Ohtani also stole two bases. And he set a Dodgers record by driving in 10 runs.

BABE RUTH

Before Ohtani, Babe Ruth was the greatest pitcher/slugger combo in MLB history. Ruth won 87 games pitching for the Red Sox from 1915 to 1919. He also broke the MLB record with 29 home runs in 1919.

Ruth moved to the Yankees in 1920. In his first year there, he blasted a record 54 home runs. The next year, he raised it to 59. And in 1927, Ruth hit 60 homers. That record stood until 1961.

THE CURSE OF THE BAMBINO

Babe Ruth began his career with the Boston Red Sox. "The Bambino" helped Boston win three World Series between 1915 and 1918. But the owner of the Red Sox needed money. He sold Ruth to the Yankees for $100,000. The Red Sox wouldn't win another World Series until 2004. Many fans called the 86-year drought "the Curse of the Bambino."

» Multiple exposures capture Sandy Koufax's powerful pitching form in action during a 1962 game.

SANDY KOUFAX

Southpaw Sandy Koufax joined the Dodgers in 1955 at age 19. He was a hard thrower, but he had problems controlling his pitches. As he matured, Koufax became one of the best pitchers in MLB history. He led MLB in strikeouts four times and in ERA and wins three times. Koufax won three NL Cy Young Awards, given to the league's top pitcher.

Highest Single-Season Batting Averages Since 1941

Red Sox left fielder Ted Williams finished the 1941 season with a .406 batting average. No MLB player has hit .400 over a full season since then. Check out how the top current MLB players have stacked up against Williams.

YEAR	MLB BATTING CHAMPION	BATTING AVERAGE
2024	**Bobby Witt** Kansas City Royals	.332
2023	**Luis Arráez** Miami Marlins	.354
2022	**Jeff McNeil** New York Mets	.326
2021	**Trea Turner** Los Angeles Dodgers	.328
2020	**DJ LeMahieu** New York Yankees	.364

MOST CAREER HOME RUNS

Babe Ruth retired in 1935 with 714 career homers. That remained the record for almost 40 years.

In 1974, Braves outfielder Hank Aaron passed Ruth with his 715th homer.

»Aaron answers questions during a press conference after surpassing Babe Ruth's record.

In 2024, the player with the most homers was Giancarlo Stanton of the New York Yankees with 429.

Retired by Multiple Teams

Many legendary players have had their numbers retired. That means no player on that team will ever wear that number again. Some players are legends in multiple cities. These players have had their numbers retired by more than one team.

Frank Robinson
Reds, Orioles, and Cleveland

Rod Carew
Twins and Angels

Hank Aaron
Braves and Brewers

Reggie Jackson
#9 Athletics, #44 Yankees

Rollie Fingers
Athletics and Brewers

Carlton Fisk
#27 Red Sox, #72 White Sox

Greg Maddux
Cubs and Braves

Gil Hodges
Mets and Dodgers

Wade Boggs
#12 Rays, #26 Red Sox

Roy Halladay
#32 Blue Jays, #34 Phillies

Willie Mays
Giants and Mets

Nolan Ryan
#30 Angels, #34 Astros, and Rangers

Jackie Robinson's jersey was retired by every team in MLB, because he broke the color barrier.

Record Breakers

CAL RIPKEN, IRONMAN

Cal Ripken debuted with the Baltimore Orioles in 1981. On May 30, 1982, he started at third base against the Toronto Blue Jays. He was in Baltimore's starting lineup every day for the next 16 seasons! Ripken broke Lou Gehrig's record of 2,130 consecutive games on September 6, 1995. But he didn't stop there. He finally took a day off on September 19, 1998. Ripken's streak of 2,632 consecutive games is not likely to be challenged.

Career Home Run Leaders

HOME RUNS	PLAYER
762	Barry Bonds
755	Henry Aaron
714	Babe Ruth
703	Albert Pujols
696	Alex Rodriguez

Top 5 Active Home Run Leaders as of March 2025

HOME RUNS	PLAYER
429	Giancarlo Stanton
378	Mike Trout
362	Paul Goldschmidt
343	Freddie Freeman
342	Manny Machado

Giancarlo Stanton

Luis Arráez

Arráez's Rise

Luis Arráez is a line-drive machine. He also doesn't strike out much. Arráez set a unique record in 2024. He became the **first player** to win **three straight batting titles** with **three different teams**.

- Arráez posted the AL's top average of .316 with the Twins in 2022.
- After being traded to the Marlins, he hit .354 in Miami to lead the NL in 2023.
- In 2024, Arráez was traded to the Padres. His .314 average led the NL that year too.

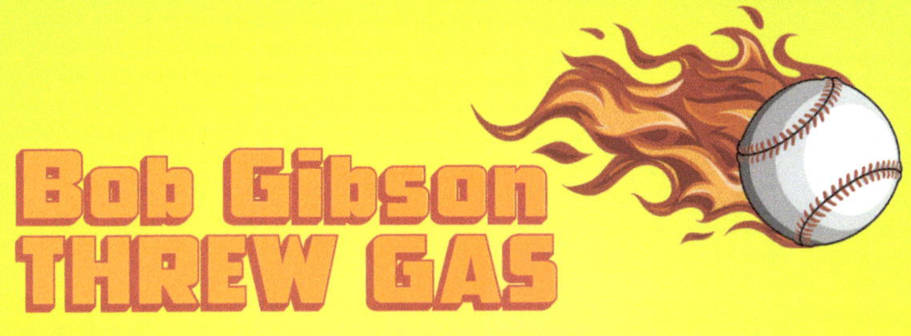

Bob Gibson THREW GAS

In 1968, **Bob Gibson** was the most dominant pitcher in the world. The Cardinals' hard-throwing right-hander won 22 games. He threw 13 shutouts. And his ERA was 1.12. As of 2024, **Chris Sale** of the Atlanta Braves had the lowest ERA of active MLB players at 2.38.

Chris Sale

DiMaggio's Streak

In 1941, Joe DiMaggio had at least one hit in 56 games in a row. Over those 56 games, DiMaggio hit .408 with 15 home runs and 55 RBIs. Nobody has come close to breaking his record.

Longest Hitting Streaks Since 1941

HITS	PLAYER AND TEAM	YEAR
56	Joe DiMaggio, Yankees	1941
44	Pete Rose, Reds	1978
39	Paul Molitor, Brewers	1987
38	Jimmy Rollins, Phillies	2005–06
37	Tommy Holmes, Braves	1945
35	Chase Utley, Phillies	2006
35	Luis Castillo, Marlins	2002
34	Dom DiMaggio, Red Sox	1949
34	Benito Santiago, Padres	1987

Jimmy Rollins

A TERROR ON THE BASEPATHS

Rickey Henderson set a record during the 1982 season with 130 stolen bases. Henderson retired as MLB's all-time stolen base king with 1,406. That's almost 500 more than any other player! Of today's players, Starling Marte of the New York Mets has the most stolen bases. At the end of 2024, he had 354 stolen bases out of 452 attempts.

» Starling Marte of the New York Mets steals second base during a 2024 game.

The Ryan Express

Nolan Ryan's fastball was called "The Ryan Express." It steamed toward the plate like a bullet train. Ryan threw seven no-hitters in his 27-year MLB career. That's three more than any pitcher in MLB history.

At the close of the 2024 season, the closest active player to Ryan's record was Justin Verlander with three no-hitters.

About the Author

Patrick Donnelly is a sportswriter and author who lives in Minneapolis, Minnesota. He's written more than 100 books about sports. He also frequently covers Minnesota sports teams for the Associated Press.

More in This Series

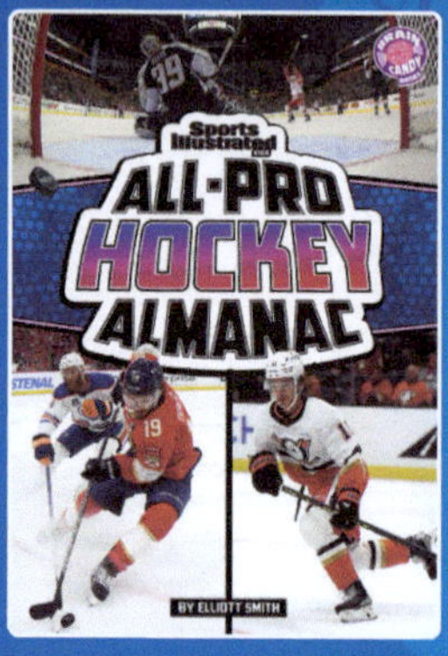

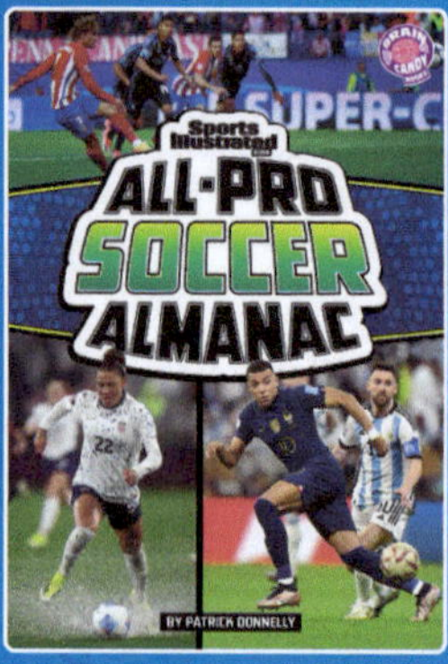